How to Dunk Like a Pro

The No-Bullshit Guide to Jumping Higher Regardless of Age or Height

By Jason Wilhelm

Table of Contents

Introduction

I want to thank you and congratulate you for purchasing *"How to Dunk Like a Pro: The No-Bullshit Guide to Jumping Higher Regardless of Age or Height."*

This book contains proven steps and strategies outlining how you can train to improve your jumping prowess, allowing you to reach the ring and dunk a basketball – irrespective of your age or height.

Too many of us believe that our ability to dunk is dictated entirely by either our height or our age (or a combination of both) – creating the misconception that there is absolutely nothing we can do to improve it.

Which, of course, is completely untrue.

In this book, I will outline time-proven strategies that you can implement into your training that will greatly improve your vertical jumping ability, making it easier for you to reach the ring and dunk like a pro.

Thanks again for purchasing this book. I hope you enjoy it!

How to Dunk a Basketball: The Ultimate Guide to Increasing Your Vertical Jump

Dunking a basketball is arguably one of the most impressive demonstrations in sport (and I mean *any* sport). To actually jump over an opponent and slam the ball requires brute strength and a *huge* amount of explosive power, combined with both an abundance of skill and finesse.

Interestingly, what many don't realize is that the ability to dunk is not necessarily a result of your skill on a basketball court alone – and it is not certainly a result of your height or age.

In fact, our ability to dunk a basketball is entirely dictated by our vertical jumping power. To actually dunk a basketball, we need to reach the ring easily and efficiently, irrespective of skill level.

This means that for us to be capable of dunking a basketball, we really need to have the physical capacity to produce power (at an extremely rapid rate) through the muscles of the legs.[1]

For this reason, our capacity to dunk a basketball is actually built in the gym – not necessarily on the court.

Taking this into consideration, dunking is essentially the final result of us taking the time to train and develop the four key physical qualities that underpin jumping performance (which I will outline in depth in our following chapters).

With this in mind, this e-book will outline how you can achieve the ability to dunk a basketball quickly and effectively by clearly outlining the training methods required to improve your vertical jump.

This will take into consideration not only those exercises that are absolutely essential to maximizing jump performance, but how we should load them and how they should be structured within a single training session – the result of which is the ultimate guide to increasing your vertical jump.

Chapter 1

What Factors Contribute to a Huge Vertical Jump (And Your Ability to Dunk a Basketball)?

There are four key factors to consider that contribute to a large vertical jump – and through that, our ability to dunk a basketball.

We will touch on each factor very briefly in this section, after which we will elaborate in much greater detail, providing explanations on both their relative importance and the best ways we can train to improve them.

1. Relative Strength – the maximal force we can produce relative to our own body weight.

2. Loaded Explosive Power – the ability to produce force rapidly under light and moderate external loads.

3. Unloaded Explosive Power – the ability to produce power completely unloaded (in which we use our own body weight as resistance).

4. Jumping Performance – the skill required to coordinate explosive power and rapid force production into jumping ability and dunk technique.

By focusing on developing these factors in isolation, we can lay a solid foundation upon which a *huge* vertical jump can be built – and it is this foundation that will help us reach the ring and dunk a basketball.

All these factors are incredibly important in their own right, and as such, they should hold a specific and independent place within your training regimen.

Although it is important to note that these factors can be (and typically are) trained in isolation, they come together collectively to produce vertical jumping power. As such, each individual factor is just as important as the next.

Chapter 2
Relative Strength and Vertical Jumping Ability

When most of us think of vertical jump training, we tend to consider fancy techniques that involve lots of high box jumps, hurdle skips, and plyometric exercises. While I certainly agree that these exercises should have a place in most vertical jump training programs, they should not always be our priority.

In fact, for these sorts of explosive exercises to have any use at all, we first need to ensure we have developed a solid foundation of strength.[2]

You see, the vertical jump is essentially a demonstration of power – which is in turn our ability to produce force at a rapid rate.

If we take this a step further, muscular power (and essentially jumping power) is therefore a combination of our maximal force-producing capacity (or in layman's terms, our strength) and the speed at which we can produce this force.

So with all this in mind, if we don't have much force to produce in the first place, the amount of force we can produce *rapidly* will obviously be limited.[2]

This ultimately describes why strength training is so important when it comes to producing a large vertical jump – it provides us with the foundation from which we can build explosive power.

A note on relative strength

I should note that there is a very specific reason why I have used the term "relative strength" specifically in this section, as opposed to the term "strength" alone.

This is because while we do want to increase our absolute strength, we want to do it without increasing our body weight too significantly. This means that our strength *relative to our current body weight* will increase – which is much more important.

This holds much more importance to our ability to dunk, because the vertical jump is highly dependent on our ability to move our own body weight (and not simply shift some big weights).

Relative strength training

Considering all this, strength training is something that should take place within a gym space – where it revolves around what most of us would consider "traditional strength training" methods.

While many may suggest that strength training is not the answer (they may even go as far as to suggest you will get too big and bulky), I can assure you that they would be very, very wrong.

Strength training has been shown time and time again to lead to big improvements in our ability to produce muscular power.[3]

Heavy strength training causes two key adaptations within the body that greatly contribute to vertical jumping ability.[4]

First, it causes significant increases in the size of our muscle fibers. To put it simply, the larger our muscle fibers are, the greater capacity they have to produce force. Through these muscular adaptations, we immediately increase the amount of force we can produce.[4]

Second, strength training also causes a big increase in the efficiency of our nervous system. This means it recruits the muscle fibers required to produce force much more efficiently – the result of which is an increase in both the amount of force we can produce and in the rate that we can produce that force.[5]

Taking these two key factors into consideration, strength training alone has been shown to lead to big improvements in vertical jumping ability – even without the addition of power-based exercises and specific jump-based training.[6]

This Which should demonstrate the importance that strength training plays in developing our ability to dunk!

Best Strength Training Exercises

It may seem a little obvious, but it is important to note that there are some exercises that are much better than others when it comes to maximizing vertical jump performance.

First, we need to prioritize lower body exercises that allow us to move an appreciable amount of weight.

This ultimately means that squat variations are going to be our best bet. With this, I typically recommend that you prioritize the barbell front squat as your primary strength exercise, simply because this movement better replicates the body's position during jumping movements in which an upright torso is maintained.[2]

Second, we need to include some single-leg strength exercises.

This means we should also include split squat variations into our training regimen. These exercises are a fantastic way to eliminate any muscular imbalances we may have, while also contributing to improving core strength.[7]

From a more "sport specific" perspective, it is quite rare in a game of basketball that we actually get the opportunity to jump off of both legs simultaneously, and as such, building single-leg strength has direct carryover to single-leg jumping ability.

How do we load these exercises?

OSo our best loading methods for these specific exercises is to use relatively heavy loads withfor lower reps.

T loading parameters maximize the development of the neuromuscular system, which as we now w, is essential to increasing force production. Through the use of heavier loads, the body becomes increasingly capable of recruiting muscle fibers, which is essential to the development of a large vertical jump.

For bilateral movements such as the front squat, I typically recommend using 4-6 sets of 3-5 repetitions. Similarly, for single-leg movements, I recommend 3-4 sets of 6-8 repetitions.

Chapter 3
Developing Explosive Power under Load

As I have already discussed at length, our ability to jump is dictated by our *ability to produce force rapidly*.

Through strength training, we can greatly improve the maximal force we can produce – but we can further enhance this by training ourselves to improve this newfound force rapidly.[8]

And this is where loaded power training enters the equation.

Loaded Power Training

Loaded power training describes exercises built around moving light and moderate weights at an extremely rapid pace.

Using Olympic weightlifters as an example: these guys (and girls) are the perfect demonstration of what loaded power training can do.

It may seem obvious, but the bulk of their training revolves around using the Olympic lifts (namely the snatch and the clean and jerk) to build explosive muscular power.

These same Olympic lifters (with specific emphasis on those in lower weight classes) are renowned for having absurdly large vertical jumps, despite rarely using unloaded jump-based exercises in their training.[1]

This provides a very nice example of how loaded power training can contribute to building and developing dunking ability.

I should add that loaded power training is somewhat similar to strength-based training in that performing these types of exercises has been shown to greatly improve the nervous system's ability to recruit muscle fibers quickly and efficiently – the result of which is a *huge* increase in the rate at which we can improve force (referred to as "rate of force development").[9]

I should note that this type of training is not particularly effective at building muscle tissue or increasing our maximal force-producing capacity *on its own* – which is why it is the perfect complement to our more traditional methods of strength training.

Loaded power training has been shown to lead to substantial improvements in vertical jump height, even without the inclusion of strength training.

I should note that this type of training appears to result in greater improvements in vertical jump in stronger individuals – which reinforces the benefits of ensuring we have a solid foundation of strength from which to build our explosive jumping power.[10]

Best Loaded Power Training Exercises

There is a myriad of different ways we can implement loaded power training into our workouts, some of which I have already touched on very briefly in the form of Olympic lifting.

The Olympic lifts and their many variations are arguably the most effective way to develop explosive jumping power using loaded power training, as to merely complete the movement correctly requires us to move a substantial amount of weight at an extremely rapid rate.

Now with this, the Olympic lifts specifically do have a bit of a downside.

They are quite technical in nature, and therefore can take a fairly large amount of time to learn. It is for this reason I recommend using slightly less technical variations of these lifts – namely the power clean and the hang power clean (performed from a "hang" position, where the bars starts above the knee).[11]

Each of these are what most would consider "regressions" of the full Olympic lifts because they are essential only a part of the movement, and they don't place the body under as much technical demand.

In conjunction with these, I also recommend the use of loaded jump squats and speed deadlifts.

Each of these utilize the same principles as the Olympic lifts (where we are moving moderate weights rapidly), and therefore result in similar adaptations in muscle power, but are much less technical in nature.[12]

As such, by using a combination of these lifts in conjunction with the other training methods outlined in this e-book, we can cover all our bases and maximize the development of our vertical jump.

How do we load these exercises?

As mentioned previously, these exercises differ significantly compared to our more traditional modes of strength training in that they require us to use light to moderate weights and move them very explosively.

In terms of loading, this means that we should be performing these movements for low reps – even despite their low relative weight.

This is because when it comes to these sorts of explosive movements, fatigue will actually limit our ability to express power, and will therefore blunt the potential training adaptations associated.

This is the primary reason I recommend using 3-5 sets of 3-5 repetitions for both Olympic lifts, speed deadlifts, and jump squats – with each rep performed as fast and as explosively as humanly possible.

With each of these movements, each rep should be just as explosive as the one that come before it. If we find ourselves slowing down toward the end of a set, it is very likely that the weight we are using is too heavy – and as a result, the training will be less effective.

Chapter 4

Unloaded Muscular Power and the Vertical Jump

While strength training and loaded power exercises are integral to maximizing the physical qualities that underpin jumping ability (and as such, our vertical jumping prowess), there is still much more we can do to increase our capacity to dunk like a pro.

And this relates to the development of our unloaded muscular power – which is closely related to jumping specifically.

Unloaded power training

Essentially unloaded muscular power is exactly what it sounds like – our ability to produce explosive power without any additional load, during which our own body weight acts as the primary source of resistance.

With this in mind, the importance this holds to jumping performance should be obvious, as it essentially describes jumping in its simplest form!

This type of training can be further broken down into two distinct categories: jump-based exercises and plyometric exercises.[13]

Jump-Based Exercises

Jump-based exercises revolve around improving our ability to produce force rapidly from a standing start. This type of training can greatly improve our rate of force development from a stationary position, which comes from an increase in the rate that the nervous system recruits muscle fibers.

By increasing this rate of recruitment, our muscles begin to reach maximal contraction much faster – the result of which is a huge spike in muscular power and jump performance.[14]

Plyometric Exercises

Plyometric exercises use the same sort of loading parameters as jump-based training (which uses our own body weight), but revolve around improving the body's capacity to utilize the stretch shortening cycle.

The stretch shortening cycle describes the contraction we observe when a muscle lengthens rapidly (in which it absorbs and stores elastic energy), and then proceeds to contract explosively (using that elastic energy to increase force production).[13]

The more developed this system is, the more effective we become at using the stretch shortening cycle. As we become more effective at utilizing this cycle, we can convert more and more of this elastic energy into concentric force – making ourselves more powerful and explosive in the process.

This becomes increasingly important during jump-based tasks that involve both landing and jumping in rapid succession – such as when we dunk a basketball.

With all this in mind, it is important to reiterate that both jump-based and plyometric exercises have proven highly effective at improving jump performance by causing large increases in jump height.

Although it is worth noting that similar to loaded power-based exercises, they appear to be more effective at improving jump performance in individuals who have a solid foundation of strength already developed – which makes it a fantastic addition to the other training modalities outlined within this program.

Best Unloaded Power Exercises

As previously mentioned, our primary exercises will fall into two distinct (but highly related) categories.

For our jump-based exercises, we can use specific exercises that closely replicate the joint angles that occur during a vertical jump. This means that box jumps, single-leg box jumps, and standing broad jumps will be our best options.

If we break it down specifically, box jumps will provide us with an excellent way to improve our explosive muscular power using both legs simultaneously, while single-leg box jumps will do the same using a single leg – both of which are likely to occur during more basketball-specific scenarios.[15]

While the action of the broad jump is not directly related to a vertical jump (since we are jumping horizontally rather than vertically), it is a movement that greatly overloads the muscles of the posterior chain (think glutes and hamstrings).

These muscles are incredibly important in all aspects of jump performance, and by increasing their force-producing capacity, we are likely to see a subsequent increase in vertical jump height.

When it comes to our plyometric-based movements, we need to focus on those that allow us to both absorb and produce force rapidly. Taking this into consideration, we need to prioritize the use of depth jumps, tuck jumps, and single-leg bounds as our primary forms of plyometric exercise.[13]

Each of these movements requires us to absorb a large amount of landing force and quickly turn it into explosive jumping power – perfectly replicating the demands placed on the lower body during dunking.

How do we load these exercises?

With both jump-based and plyometric exercises, the same considerations need to be taken – and they are very similar to the loaded power exercises we discuss at length in chapter 3.

By this, we mean we do not want to train them until we are fatigued, as this will seriously inhibit their effectiveness.

It is very much quality over quantity with these types of movement, in which each individual repetition is performed as quickly and as explosively as possible – enhancing the efficiency of the nervous system and greatly increasing its ability to recruit muscle fibers without the addition of load.

With these, I would recommend these exercises being performed for no more than 3-4 sets of 3-5 repetitions.

This will ensure they are not performed to fatigue, thus providing us with the greatest degree of adaptation.

Chapter 5
Specifically Training Jump Performance to Improve Dunk Technique.

Throughout the previous three chapters, we have essentially discussed the steps we need take to ensure we develop the physical qualities that underpin jump performance from every angle.

This is done by increasing our maximal force-producing capacity (through strength training), training our ability to produce force rapidly (through loaded power training), and improving the nervous system's ability to utilize the stretch shortening cycle effectively (through unloaded power training).

All of these are absolutely essential to develop our capacity to jump explosively and jump high.

But none of these will actually improve our dunking technique – which is exactly where jumping performance training comes into play.[17]

Jumping Performance Training

This type of training revolves more closely around the technical aspects of jump performance, in which we want to take the time to hone our dunking technique, making it as effective and efficient as possible.

This type of training differs significantly from the others outlined in this book as it is ultimately skill dependent and should therefore be trained on separate days if possible.

In terms of training adaptations, these types of exercises prepare us mentally and physically for the act of dunking on the court, rather than developing strength and power specifically.

And although it may not sound all that exciting, it is incredibly important, as it essentially links all the essential gym-based training adaptations to basketball-specific performance.

Jump performance training

TNow this sort of training revolves around on- court performance and essentially relates to the skill-based practice of both your run- up and your dunking action.

Tare two primary dunking actions undertakn by basketball athletes: a single-leg take-off, and a double-leg take-off.

Dunking using a single-leg take-off is arguably an easier skill to learn, as the movement itself comes more naturally to a lot of people. I believe that this is because the movement pattern required to perform this type of dunk very closely replicates a typical lay-up technique – making the associated learning curve much less steep.

A dunk using a double-leg take off can be a lot more difficult to learn, and often feels less natural to many athletes. Despite that, this type of dunk is arguably the more spectacular of the two, and is worth learning if you have the time to commit to developing the skills required.

Dunking with a single-leg takeoff

As mentioned previously, this technique is easier to learn as it more closely replicates traditional lay-up technique in which we simply run up the ring at an angle, jumping off of one leg (often the leg closest to the ring) while reaching for the rim with our hand (opposite the foot we jumped off).

For most right-handers, this means running at the ring from left of court, jumping off of your left foot and reaching for the ring with your right hand.

A few things that are very important to note is that in this scenario, *speed matters*.

Too many people come toward the ring and then slow down drastically. This loss of acceleration greatly limits the amount of power we can produce, and therefore negatively impacts our vertical jump height.

By instead maintaining pace, we will maintain speed and acceleration, and we will jump much higher as a result.

Using this technique, it is also incredibly important that we pay close attention to the penultimate step.

The penultimate step describes the second to last step we take prior to takeoff, in which its correct performance is essential for a successful dunk. As we approach the ring, it is important that we lower our center of gravity during this step, converting our speed into elastic energy that we can then use to maximize our jump performance.

The stride length of this step is likely to be a little longer than the steps that come before it, allowing you to use a vertical jumping action on your final step, greatly increasing your vertical leap as a result.

A dunk using a single-leg takeoff is convenient as it can be performed quickly, increasing your ability to avoid blocks – and as we can typically jump farther off a single leg, this technique can also be performed when we are farther away from the ring.

Dunking with a dual-leg takeoff

When it comes the spectacular dunks, most of us think of those with a double-leg takeoff (often involving the individual launching themselves over the top of an opponent).

In this scenario, you are required to come toward the ring with your body facing toward it, and this is essential, since we are going to use both hands to dunk the ball.

We are still required to approach the ring at full speed, but during our penultimate step, we dip down at the legs (lowering our body's center of gravity) while simultaneously swinging our arms down toward the ground – maximizing our storage of elastic energy.

From here, we explode up, launching ourselves off of both feet at the exact same time.

This technique requires you to be slightly closer to the ring than its single-legged counterpart, and as such, can actually be performed from a standstill if you have the strength and power to do so (I should note that it is still much easier to perform with a quick run-up).

As an added bonus, these jumps tend to place less load on the ankles and the knees, although they do require more time to perform, making them easier to block in the process.

Steps to improving jump performance and dunking technique

This is actually quite simple, and it comes down to one word: practice.

These sorts of jumps are a skill, and as a result, they improve through repeated practice. As such, every time you step on a court, you should spend a significant portion of time practicing your jumps and working on your dunking technique. This will greatly improve your dunking ability, ensuring all the hard training you have put in is worth it.

A point worth making is that some people do find using a smaller ball (such as a tennis or lacrosse ball) easier in the initial stages, since these are easier to control. As a result, you can spend more time focusing on your run-up and dunking technique without worrying about ball control.

As you become more competent and your dunk technique becomes more autonomic, you can slowly build toward using a full-sized basketball.

Chapter 6
Putting It All Together – The Ultimate Vertical Jump Training Program.

Now that we have taken the time to establish what aspects of performance we need to focus on (and why we need to focus on them), it is time to put it all together.

In this chapter, I have provided a three day per week training program that will lead to the greatest improvements in your vertical jumping ability – ensuring that you can dunk effectively.

Each of these sessions should be separated by at least one rest day where you do not attend the gym. For example, completing the sessions on Monday Wednesday, and Friday, or Tuesday, Thursday, and Saturday, would be perfect.

While this program is designed to last eight weeks (broken down into two four-week blocks), it can be run over and over again to see continual improvements in strength, power, and jumping ability – making it easier and easier for you to dunk a basketball.

With this in mind, each session has been specially structured to maximize the development of your vertical jump, and as such, I implore you to complete it exactly how it is outlined within the book.

A quick note on loading:

Also worth mentioning is how we should load the exercises outlined in the section below.

With all unloaded power exercises, we will use our own body weight as the primary form of resistance (so loading is simple). Every single rep of these exercises needs to be performed as explosively as possible – remember, with these, it is definitely quality over quantity.

All loaded power exercises need to be performed with low to moderate loads. With this, I recommend erring on the side of caution and starting quite conservative with your weight selection. Again, each rep should feel fast and explosive. If you feel like you are moving slower and slower as the set progresses, the weight you are using is too heavy.

With these exercises, adding five pounds per week should be manageable without seeing a reduction in speed.

When it comes to our strength-based exercises, things can get a little tricky.

For each exercise, I would recommend starting with a weight that you can perform for *two more reps than what is prescribed*. This will maximize safety and lead to the greatest neural adaptions.

For example, if we have five sets of five reps programmed, I would recommend starting with a weight you can perform for seven reps. This means that each set will become more and more challenging until you reach the final set, at which point you should be very close to your limit.

In a similar fashion, with those movements where you are expected to perform eight reps, I would recommend starting with a weight you can perform for 10 reps – since again, by the final set, you will be reaching your maximum threshold.

For all strength-based exercises, adding five pounds per week should be manageable and will lead to continued improvements over time – no matter how many times you run through the program.

Weeks 1-4

In the first four weeks, we will be prioritizing the development of muscular strength. This will allow us to build a solid foundation from which muscular power and explosive jumping ability will be built.

As such, it is essential that we complete this first four-week block first!

Session 1

1. **Box Jump** - 4 sets of 3 reps (60 sec rest between sets)

2. **Power Clean** - 4 sets of 4 reps (60 sec rest between sets)

3. **Speed Deadlifts** - 4 sets of 3 reps (60 sec rest between sets)

4. **Barbell Front Squat** - 5 sets of 5 reps (120 sec rest between sets)

5. **Bulgarian Split Squat** - 3 sets of 8 reps per side (120 sec rest between sets)

Session 2

1. **Single-leg Box Jump** - 4 sets of 3 reps per side (60 sec rest between sets)

2. **Hang Clean** - 4 sets of 4 reps (60 sec rest between sets)

3. **Barbell Back Squat** - 5 sets of 3 reps (120 sec rest between sets)

4. **Dumbbell Split Squat** - 3 sets of 8 reps per side (120 sec rest between sets)

Session 3

1. **Broad Jumps** - 4 sets of 4 reps (60 sec rest between sets)

2. **Loaded Jump Squats** - 4 sets of 3 reps (60 sec rest between sets)

3. **Barbell Front Squats** - 5 sets of 4 reps (120 sec rest between sets)

4. **Reverse Lunges** - 3 sets of 8 reps per side (120 sec rest between sets)

Weeks 5-8

Once we have developed a solid foundation of strength, it is time to increase our explosive power performance. The primary focus of this four-week block is to improve our rate of force development, leading to increased muscular power, which in turn leads to a greatly enhanced jump height.

I should note that there will also be some strength exercises included in each session. This will ensure we maintain (and even improve upon) the relative strength we have spent the previous four weeks developing, while further enhancing our maximal force-producing capabilities.

Session 1

1. **Depth Jumps** - 4 sets of 4 reps (60 sec rest between sets)

2. **Single-Leg Hops** - 4 sets of 4 reps per side (60 sec rest between sets)

3. **Loaded Squat Jumps** - 3 sets of 3 reps (60 sec rest between sets)

4. **Power Clean** - 3 sets of 4 reps (75 sec rest between sets)

5. **Barbell Front Squat** - 6 sets of 3 reps (120 sec rest between sets)

Session 2

1. **Tuck Jump** - 5 sets of 3 reps (60 sec rest between sets)

2. **Single-Leg Box Jumps** - 4 sets of 3 reps per side (60 sec rest between sets)

3. **Hang Clean** - 5 sets of 3 reps (60 sec rest between sets)

4. **Bulgarian Split Squat** - 5 sets of 5 reps per side (120 sec rest between sets)

5. **Dumbbell Split Squat** - 4 sets of 6 reps per side (120 sec rest between sets)

Session 3

1. **Repeated Broad Jumps** - 5 sets of 3 reps (60 sec rest between sets)

2. **Depth Jumps** - 4 sets of 3 reps (60 sec rest between sets)

3. **Box Jumps** - 5 sets of 3 reps (60 sec rest between sets)

4. **Speed Deadlifts** - 5 sets of 4 reps (90 sec rest between sets)

5. **Barbell Front Squat** - 6 sets of 2 reps (120 sec rest between sets)

A note about rest days

Ideally, we would have rest days in between our gym-based training days. Having this time will allow the body to recover from the previous day's session, promoting muscular adaption, which is integral to improving our performance in the long run.

But with this in mind, there are certain things you can do on your rest days if you feel up to it.

First, you are more than welcome to undertake some light aerobic activity. Whether this is a light jog, a casual swim, or an easy ride, this is all fine. Performing this type of cardiovascular exercise is a great way to promote blood flow to the muscle tissue, increasing our rate of recovery (while also improving our cardiovascular fitness).

Second, you could take some time and practice your jump performance and specific dunk technique. This will give you an opportunity to apply all the training-induced improvements in strength and power you have developed to your on-court performance.

And finally, you can also do some upper body exercises in the gym (especially if that is something you enjoy doing). As long as we give the muscle tissue of the lower body time to recover between sessions, performing upper body exercises will not limit your progress in the slightest.

Chapter 7
Warming Up For Your Training Sessions

Now that we have a thorough understanding of how we need to train to see some monster improvements in vertical jump and dunking ability, it is also important that we spend a bit of time discussing how to warm up effectively.

I would go as far as to suggest that the warm-up is underutilized 99% of the time.

Many don't realize this, but merely going for a light jog before we commence exercises does not describe an effective warm-up. While it will increase blood flow throughout the body, that is all it does – and to maximize both our performance *and* the effectiveness of our training, we need much more than that.

An effective warm up should improve our available range of motion at specific joints, activate the primary muscles involved in the upcoming session, and prepared us for the movements outlined in the upcoming session.

With this in mind, our warm-ups will be broken down into four key stages: release, mobilization, activation, and movement preparation.

Release

The first part of our warm-up revolves around improving the range of motion we have available at our joints *and* improving the tissue quality of our muscle – both of which can be done through the use of a concept known as Self-Myofascial Release (or SMR for short).[17]

SMR essentially describes a massage that we give ourselves, which can be done using a tennis ball, or more commonly, a foam roller. Using these tools, we can massage tight tissue and cause it to release, which in turn increases our joint range of motion.[18]

With this, we want to focus on those muscles around the hip and the ankle specifically, as it is these muscles that receive a heap of work during both lower body strength exercises and jumping movements. Subsequently, it is these muscles that generally get tight and restricted as a result.[18]

Keeping with this trend, our primary focus will be on the calves, quads, adductors, and glutes.

Mobilization

During the second part of our warm-up, we want to focus on increasing the range of motion available at our joints and then mobilizing those joints.

In doing so, we can improve our ability to get into more demanding positions, while also making it easier to perform large compound movements such as squats, split squats, and deadlifts.

This is going to have a host of positive effects, in which we will both improve our ability to perform those movements during our gym-based training sessions (increasing our performance in the long run), *and* reduce our risk of injury during sport performance specifically.[19]

This can be accomplished through two primary means: static stretching and dynamic mobility exercises.

Static Stretching

Static stretching has copped a heap of negative attention over the last few years due to some interesting research suggesting it can limit power production.

While I won't discredit this research (since stretching can inhibit strength and power somewhat when performed for extremely long durations), static stretching does offer an excellent way to improve the length of our muscle tissue – and as such, it is the perfect complement to SMR when it comes to increasing flexibility and improving tissue quality.[18]

The way we physically perform static stretching can greatly improve the results, particularly if we are performing it immediately before a training session.

With this in mind, rather than holding each individual stretch for a very long duration, I would recommend "pulsing" in and out of the stretch, where we move into the stretched position for five *hard* seconds and then relax for five seconds (in which this would be a single rep).

The areas of the body that respond best to stretching tend to be the hip flexors and quads.[20] As such, these muscles will be our primary focus when it comes to stretching.

Dynamic Mobility

Now that we have restored tissue quality through the use of SMR and improved the length of our muscle tissue by using pulse-driven static stretching, we can now further maximize the range of motion we have available in our joints.

By using dynamic mobility exercises to "explore" our end joint ranges, we can improve our ability use those joint ranges on a more regular basis, improving overall mobility, flexibility, and movement quality.

It is necessary to perform dynamic mobility exercises in a slow and controlled manner, wherein we "tease out" the end ranges of our joints – and in which each individual rep gets us closer and closer to our joints' end range of motion.

With these exercises, as with our other mobility exercises, we really want to target the hips, ankles, and thoracic spine, as these joints play the largest role in vertical jumping and dunking movements.

Activation

The next phase of the warm up focuses on preparing the prime movers of the body for the upcoming exercise session.

When it comes to complex movements such as box jumps, plyometric exercises, squats, deadlifts, and their single-leg variations, we are essentially using every muscle within the lower body to produce them.

Interestingly, some of those smaller muscles are not necessarily the most effective when it comes to producing a strong and powerful contraction – which is why we want to spend a little bit of time before our workout activating one of the largest muscle groups in the body: the glutes.[21]

The glutes are basically those massive muscles that essentially make up our entire backside.

If we break it down a little further, the gluteal muscle group is comprised of three distinct muscles: gluteus maximus, gluteus medius, and gluteus minimus (more commonly known as glute max, glute med, and glute min).

Of these three muscles, glute max and glute med are both the biggest and strongest – and as such, hold the most importance when it comes to maximizing performance.

It is important to note that while these two muscles are indeed part of the same muscle group, they actually play significantly different roles during movement.

Glute max is the biggest of the two muscles; it sits on the most posterior portion of the buttock. Due to its positioning, glute max plays a big role during movements that require extension of the hip joint from a flexed position.

With this in mind, when talking about real-life scenarios, glute max plays a very big role in movements such as jumping, bounding, and sprinting.

Glute med, on the other hand, sits quite laterally around the hip, where it actually produces *hip abduction* – which describes the movement of the leg laterally as it moves away from the body.

In conjunction with hip abduction, glute med also plays an incredibly important role maintaining a level and stable pelvis during single-leg stance, and as such, is integral during single-leg jumps, single-leg bounds, and short sprints.

Keeping this in mind, it is important we "activate" these two key muscles prior to commencing exercise as a way to increase their involvement during training. Doing so will improve performance and reduce the risk of injury.[21]

This will be accomplished by performing glute med and glute max isolation exercises immediately after our dynamic mobility exercises, preparing them for our upcoming session.

Movement

Our final warm-up stage revolves around performing low-level movements that replicate those we perform either in the gym or on the court.

In doing so, we greatly increase our preparedness for exercise. We will promote blood flow to the important (and now "activated") muscle tissue, which also greatly reduces our risk of developing injuries.

This means performing squat variations, split squat variations, and deadlift variations (using our body weight as our only source of resistance) to "grease" these primary movement patterns.

Putting it all together

Now that we have a thorough understanding of each of individual warm-up phase, it is time to put them together into a single package – an ultimate warm-up, if you will.

The following warm-up can be used prior to any of our lower-body sessions *or* basketball training sessions/skill sessions as a way to improve our performance and reduce our risk of injury.

SMR

1. **Foam roll quads** - 30 sec each side

2. **Foam roll adductors** - 30 sec each side

3. **Foam roll calves** - 30 sec each side

4. **Tennis ball glutes** - 30 sec each side

Stretching

1. **Half kneeling hip flexor stretch** - 10 x 5 sec pulses each side

2. **Standing quad stretch** - 10 x 5 sec pulses each side

Dynamic Mobility

1. **Half kneeling adductor rock back** - 10 reps each side

2. **Knee to wall ankle mobilization** - 10 reps each side

3. **Pull knee to chest** - 10 reps each side

Activation

1. **Prone hip extension** - 10 reps per side

2. **Side lying clams** - 10 reps per side

3. **Glute bridge** - 10 reps

Movement

1. **Body weight squat** - 10 reps

2. **Walking lunges** - 10 reps per side

3. **Single-leg deadlift** - 10 reps per side

And done!

The above warm-up should only take 8-10 minutes and will perfectly prepare you for exercise.

Chapter 8
Optimizing Your Diet for Maximal Improvements and Performance

An often-overlooked aspect of improving performance is our diet.

And that is a shame.

Because what we eat (and in what amounts) can significantly impact both the result of our training and how well we actually perform on game day (and during those training sessions).

With this in mind, the first thing we need to do is gain an understanding of the three key macronutrients and their relationship to exercise and recovery, after which we can establish what (and how much) we need to eat.

Considering this, the food we eat can essentially be broken down into three primary macronutrients (or four if we count alcohol): carbohydrates, proteins, and fats.[22]

We will touch on each of these in detail.

Carbohydrates

Carbohydrates are made up of glucose molecules, which our body breaks down to use for energy. With this in mind, the consumption of carbohydrates is essential if we have any hope of performing high-intensity physical activities (such as those outlined in this book).

To build on this further, carbohydrates can be categorized as either simple or complex.

For the sake of simplicity, complex carbohydrates typically come from things that have been grown in the ground. Whole grains, fruits, and vegetables tend to tick this box pretty well.

Complex carbohydrates are known to be absorbed from the digestive system into the blood stream quite slowly, where they provide a prolonged and sustained release of energy into the body.

Simple carbohydrates, on the other hand, typically come from processed sources such as breads, pasta, cakes, sugar, candy, and other junk foods. These types of foods are digested and absorbed by the body at an extremely rapid rate, where their consumption is often associated with a subsequent "sugar crash."[22]

It is important to note that while carbohydrates have been copping a bit of flack within the health and fitness community of late, there is nothing inherently wrong with carbohydrate consumption.

In fact, considering the important role they play in energy production, they are essential to ensuring we can perform intense exercise to the best of our abilities.

Building on this further, maintaining adequate carbohydrate consumption can increase the amount of work we perform each training session, thereby significantly improving the result of our training.

As such, we should strive to consume approximately 2-2.5 grams of carbohydrate for every pound we weigh per day. Additionally, we should to ensure 80% of our carbohydrates come from complex sources.

Protein

If carbohydrates are our fuel source, proteins are our building blocks.[22]

Protein molecules are broken down into amino acids, which are considered essential nutrients, since they play a number of important roles within the human body.

Of these roles, repairing and rebuilding damaged muscle and connective tissue is one of its most important, which is why maintaining adequate protein intake is absolutely integral to building muscle and recovering from workouts.

By increasing our rate of recovery, protein can greatly increase the effectiveness of our training, which in turn further improves the results of our training.

Protein is found in meat, poultry, eggs, dairy, nuts, seeds, grains, and legumes, and it should be an essential part of our diet if we are looking to maximize our performance.

Taking this into consideration, I recommend you try and consume approximately 1 gram of protein per pound of body weight *per day*.

Fats

While fats were once demonized within the health and fitness industry, recent research has shown that they are in fact integral to the health of our tissues at the cellular level.

In addition to this, they are also known to play an important role in the production of numerous hormones within the human body (some of which improve strength and muscle growth). They have even been shown to improve the function of our nervous system.23

Fats can be broken down into three main categories: saturated fat, monounsaturated fat, and polyunsaturated fat.

Saturated fats are found in red meat, butter, and dairy products, and actually have the potential to promote the development of lean muscle tissue by aiding in the production of testosterone (one of our most anabolic hormones).

With this in mind, a moderate intake of saturated fat combined with heavy resistance training (such as that explained in this program) has been shown to greatly increase testosterone secretion and production when combined with both increases in muscle strength and athletic performance.24

Monounsaturated are found in avocados, nuts, olive oil, and other high-fat fruits, and are often considered "healthy fats," as they have shown to reduce the amount of "bad" cholesterol in the blood while simultaneously increasing the amount of "good" cholesterol.22

Consuming some monounsaturated fats each day can therefore improve our health and function, which can further improve the effects of our training.

Finally, we have polyunsaturated fats.

Polyunsaturated fats are found in seafood, fish oil, various seeds, and soy, and like monounsaturated fats, have shown to have a positive effect on our blood cholesterol ratio while also improving the function of our cells.

Because fat has a very high energy content, I recommend you keep its intake down to approximately .5 grams per pound of body weight per day.

With this, the bulk of these should come from natural sources such as red meat, eggs, dairy, fish, avocadoes, and nuts, while very little (if any) should come from vegetable or seed oils.

A note on macronutrient timing

Now that we have a thorough understanding of each of the three primary macronutrients and why their intake is indeed essential, it is time to touch on when we should be eating them.

While I will not debate that the total amount of macronutrients we consume on a daily basis holds more importance than when we actually consume them, by placing a secondary focus on our macronutrient timing, we can take our results to the next level.

The principles behind this are simple.

The meals both immediately before and immediately after our workouts should be comprised of mostly carbohydrates and protein, but minimal fats.

This ensures that we have enough carbohydrates readily available to fuel our training sessions, while also guaranteeing that the muscles have a steady stream of amino acids available to aid recovery and muscular development.

As fat is known to slow the digestion of carbohydrates and protein, we want to keep its intake to a minimum during this time, ensuring we optimize both the energy available for our workouts and our recovery processes.

Taking this into consideration, our other meals should be comprised mostly of fats and protein. This will ensure we get a sufficient intake of these nutrients each and every day without having a negative impact on our performance or training.

An Example Day

To put it all together, in the below table I have organized an example of a daily macronutrient breakdown for a 180-pound individual who trains at 5:00 p.m.

With this, it is important to keep in mind that based upon the above recommendations, this individual should be consuming approximately 180 grams of protein, 90 grams of fat, and 360 grams of carbohydrates *each day*.

	Macronutrient (grams)		
	Protein	Carbohydrate	Fat
Meal 1 (*8am*)	50	10 – 15	40
Meal 2 (*12pm*)	50	10 – 15	5
Meal 3 (*3:30pm pre-workout*)	40	160	5
Meal 4 (*7:30pm post-workout*)	40	160	40

While this is indeed a simplistic approach, it guarantees that we have the essential nutrients available *when we need them,* which in turn improves our performance during training while also improving the *results* of our training.

Chapter 9
Training Equipment to Take Your Results to the Next Level!

I would go as far as to suggest that 95% of learning how to dunk is already described in great detail within the previous chapters of this book – most of which come with a heavy dose of both hard work and dedication.

But in saying that, there is certainly some essential equipment that can help you achieve that final 5% - which can at times be the difference between barely touching the ring and smoking a dunk.

In this final chapter, I want to outline the two pieces of equipment that I believe are essential to maximizing dunk performance.

Taking this into consideration, I won't be touching on pieces of equipment that are essential to gym-based training (such as weights and gym equipment), but rather performance-based equipment that can literally help you jump higher.

Invest in a solid pair of basketball sneakers

I do realize that this may sound a little silly (any pair of shoes should be fine, right?), but hear me out for a moment.

Basketball sneakers have been designed with both jumping and landing in mind.

First, this means that a decent pair of sneakers has the capacity to absorb force during jumping and landing movements. This greatly increases the amount of force we transfer into the ground during jumping movements, and it makes landing safer and less demanding on the joints of the body.

Secondly, these types of shoes offer a heap of stability at the ankle joint. In doing so, they greatly reduce our likelihood of developing a lower body injury, which increases our training safety tenfold. This can, in turn, result in an increase in training consistency and effect the results of our training in a positive manner as a result.

Finally, the soles of these shoes have been built with exceptional grip. This greatly reduces the risk of slipping, which further improves our ability to transfer force into the ground. It can also lead to greater jump heights and reduce the risk of injury.

A Comfortable Training Kit

When learning to jump, both in a gym setting and out on the court, it is imperative that our movements remain unrestricted. With this in mind, if we are caught wearing tight and uncomfortable clothing, our jump performance will be severely limited.

This means wearing light and loose clothing to ensure that we have the ability to move freely, which in turn ensures we can maximize our power production.

While this may sound a little obvious, being comfortable during training can greatly impact both how we train and the results of that training.

And that's it!

Seriously, some equipment is so much more important than others – and these two pieces are unquestionably the most important.

By ensuring you have a high-quality pair of basketball sneakers *and* a comfortable training kit, you can take your performance to the next level while ensuring you don't sustain any unnecessary injuries.

Conclusion

Thank you again for purchasing this book!

I hope this book was able to help you to understand what training methods will lead to the largest improvements in your dunking ability and why!

The next step is to undertake the program outlined in this book, from start to finish, with dedication and intent. In doing so you will see huge increases in strength, muscular power, and of course, vertical jump performance.

By developing these factors, you will see significant improvement in your dunk performance – getting you right up the ring!

And finally, if you did enjoy this book, then I would like to ask you a favor: would you be kind enough to <u>leave a review</u> for this book an amazon? It would be greatly appreciated!

References

1. Tricoli, Valmor, et al. "Short-term effects on lower-body functional power development: weightlifting vs. vertical jump training programs." *Journal of Strength and Conditioning Research* 19.2 (2005): 433.

2. Wisløff, U., et al. "Strong correlation of maximal squat strength with sprint performance and vertical jump height in elite soccer players." *British Journal of Sports Medicine* 38.3 (2004): 285-288.

3. Fatouros, Ioannis G., et al. "Evaluation of plyometric exercise training, weight training, and their combination on vertical jumping performance and leg strength." *The Journal of Strength & Conditioning Research* 14.4 (2000): 470-476.

4. Häkkinen, K., et al. "Neuromuscular adaptations during concurrent strength and endurance training versus strength training." *European Journal of Applied Physiology* 89.1 (2003): 42-52.

5. Sale, Digby G. "Neural adaptation to strength training." *Strength and Power in Sport, Second Edition* (2008): 281-314.

6. Baker, Daniel. "Improving vertical jump performance through general, special, and specific strength training." *Journal of Strength and Conditioning Research* 10 (1996): 131-136.

7. Andersen, V., et al. "Muscle activation and strength in squat and Bulgarian squat on stable and unstable surface." *International Journal of Sports Medicine* 35.14 (2014): 1196-1202.

8. Dugan, E. L., et al. "Determining the optimal load for jump squats: a review of methods and calculations." *Journal of Strength and Conditioning research* 18.3 (2004): 668-674.

9. Prue, P., M. R. McGuigan, and R. U. Newton. "Influence of Strength on the Magnitude & Mechanisms of Adaptation to Power Training." *Med Sci Sports Exerc* 42.8 (2010): 1566-1581.

10. Baker, Daniel, and Steven Nance. "The Relation Between Running Speed and Measures of Strength and Power in Professional Rugby League Players." *The Journal of Strength & Conditioning Research* 13.3 (1999): 230-235.

11. Kilduff, Liam P., et al. "Optimal loading for peak power output during the hang power clean in professional rugby players." *International Journal of Sports Physiology and Performance* 2.3 (2007): 260-269.

12. Hoffman, Jay R., et al. "Comparison of loaded and unloaded jump squat training on strength/power performance in college football players." *Journal of Strength and Conditioning Research* 19.4 (2005): 810.

13. Markovic, Goran. "Does plyometric training improve vertical jump height? A meta-analytical review." *British Journal of Sports Medicine* 41.6 (2007): 349-355.

14. Cormie, Prue, Jeffrey M. McBride, and Grant O. McCaulley. "Power-time, force-time, and velocity-time curve analysis of the countermovement jump: impact of training." *The Journal of Strength & Conditioning Research* 23.1 (2009): 177-186.

15. Balčiūnas, Mindaugas, et al. "Long term effects of different training modalities on power, speed, skill and anaerobic capacity in young male basketball players." *Journal of Sports Science & Medicine* 5.1 (2006): 163.

16. Starkes, Janet, et al. "Abilities and skill in basketball." *International Journal of Sport Psychology* (1994).

17. MacDonald, Graham Z., et al. "An acute bout of self-myofascial release increases range of motion without a subsequent decrease in muscle activation or force." *The Journal of Strength & Conditioning Research* 27.3 (2013): 812-821.

18. Škarabot, Jakob, Chris Beardsley, and Igor Štirn. "Comparing the effects of self-myofascial release with static stretching on ankle range-of-motion in adolescent athletes." *International Journal of Sports Physical Therapy* 10.2 (2015): 203.

19. Wang, H. K., and T. Cochrane. "Mobility impairment, muscle imbalance, muscle weakness, scapular asymmetry and shoulder injury in elite volleyball athletes." *Journal of Sports Medicine and Physical Fitness* 41.3 (2001): 403.

20. Young, Warren, et al. "Acute effects of static stretching on hip flexor and quadriceps flexibility, range of motion and foot

speed in kicking a football." *Journal of Science and Medicine in Sport* 7.1 (2004): 23-31.

21. Distefano, Lindsay J., et al. "Gluteal muscle activation during common therapeutic exercises." *Journal of Orthopaedic & Sports Physical Therapy* 39.7 (2009): 532-540.

22. Zello, Gordon A. "Dietary Reference Intakes for the macronutrients and energy: considerations for physical activity." *Applied Physiology, Nutrition, and Metabolism* 31.1 (2006): 74-79.

23. Gasior, Maciej, Michael A. Rogawski, and Adam L. Hartman. "Neuroprotective and disease-modifying effects of the ketogenic diet." *Behavioural Pharmacology* 17.5-6 (2006): 431.

24. Volek, Jeff S., et al. "Testosterone and cortisol in relationship to dietary nutrients and resistance exercise." *Journal of Applied Physiology* 82.1 (1997): 49-54.